Table of Contents

At School

At Home

Holidays

When the Bell Rings...

We slide down.

We run fast.

We wait in line.

Little Fish, Big Fish

swimming

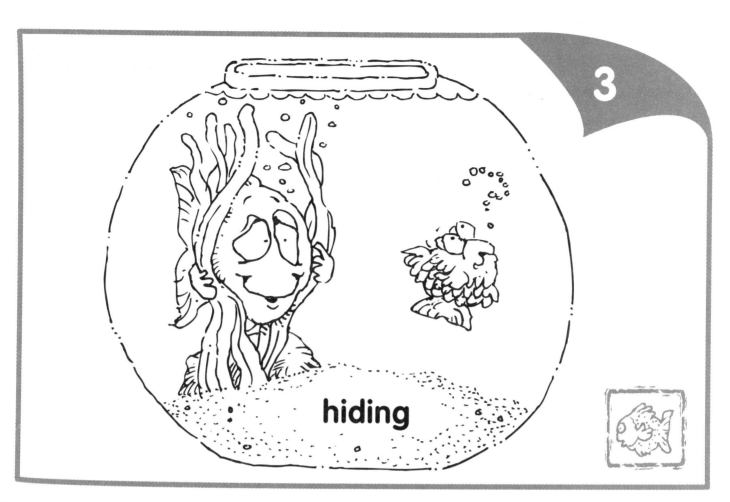

3

hiding

4

eating

5

Up and Down

Now I am up.

Now I am down.

Can you see
I'm upside down?

The Chalkboard

Our teacher writes on the chalkboard.

Our helper writes on the chalkboard.

I write on the chalkboard, too.

On the Playground

the swing, the bars

10

the basket, the balls

the kids

Snack Time

a carrot, a cookie, some juice

a marshmallow treat and grapes

ants on a log or bananas

Snacks come in many shapes.

Painting

First the red.

Then the blue.

Oops---How about purple?

Circle Time

We listen. We talk.

We sing. We dance.

We think. We learn.

Fifty Little Stories to Read EMC 743

Sharing Time

Ivan brought his bear to share.

Sophie brought her skates to share.

I brought my baby brother to share.

The Water Table

Dip and pour.

Have some more.

Mop the floor.

The Guest

**Yesterday he came to school.
He rode in Sammy's vest.**

Fifty Little Stories to Read EMC 743

He jumped into our circle.
He did his very best.

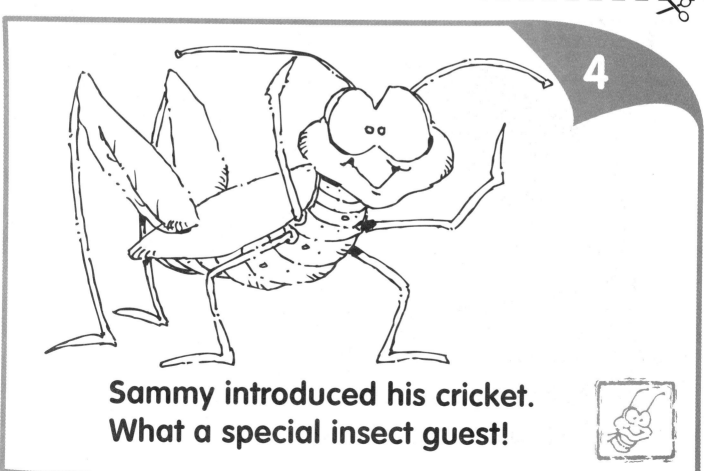

Sammy introduced his cricket.
What a special insect guest!

The Secret

Annie told Mike.

Then Mike told Sue.

Sue told Scott and Peter, too..

Peter told Ray. Scott told Saul.
It isn't very secret at all!

Fifty Little Stories to Read EMC 743

The Library

Big books. Little books.

 Fifty Little Stories to Read EMC 743

Thick books. Skinny books.

I love books!

Sand

Fill it up.

Fifty Little Stories to Read EMC 743

Sand in the pail.

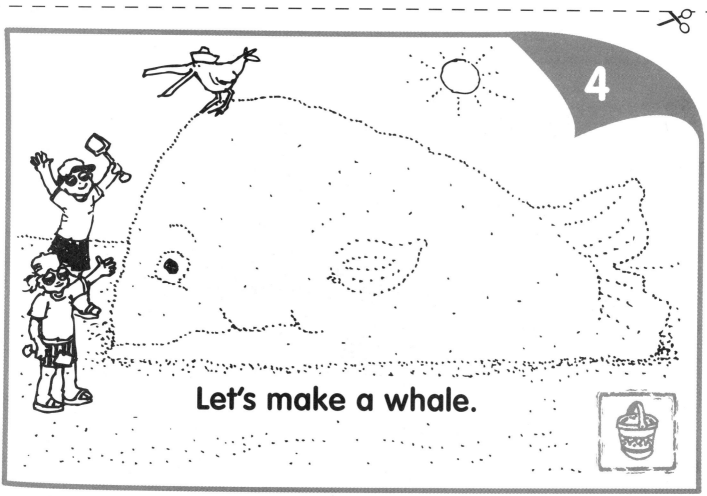

Let's make a whale.

My Computer

My computer helps me draw.

The dog can dig.

My computer helps me write.

The dog can dig.

My computer helps me read.

My computer helps me learn.

Thanks, Computer.

Our Friends—
The Fire Fighters

See the fire trucks.
They roar down the street.

The fire fighters put the fire out.
They help the people.
They rescue pets.

They help us learn how to keep fires
from starting in the first place.

 Fifty Little Stories to Read EMC 743

Different Is OK

We are both five years old,
but we are different.

I have blue eyes.
You have brown eyes.

I have curly hair.
Your hair is straight.

My skin is dark. My skin is light.

36

I like pizza.
So do I.

We are the same and we
are different and that's ok!

The New Kid

A new kid came to school today.
He had a red striped hat.

I sat beside him and ate my snack.
He let me share his mat.

We played together with the blocks.
We had a little chat.

I think that we'll be new best friends.
What do you think of that?

Growing

Growing taller.

Growing stronger.

40

Growing smarter.

Growing longer.

The Puddle

1

Raindrops splash in the puddle.

2

Fifty Little Stories to Read EMC 743

Puppies splash in the puddle.

I splash in the puddle, too!

Hurry Up!

Hurry up. It's time to go.

Hurry up. It's time to go.

Hurry up! It's time to go!

Good Night

Little bird, it's time for bed.

Little kitty, it's time for bed.

Little girl, it's time for bed.

 Fifty Little Stories to Read EMC 743

It's Time for Bed

Brush your teeth.

It's time for bed. Get on your pjs.

48 *Fifty Little Stories to Read EMC 743*

It's time for bed. Let's read a story.

It's time for bed. Turn off the light.

Fifty Little Stories to Read EMC 743

My Growing Team

My doctor helps me grow.

My dentist helps me grow.

My teacher helps me grow.

I'm Ready To Go!

1

I can zip zippers.

2

I can button buttons.

3

I can buckle buckles.

4

I can snap snaps.

Fifty Little Stories to Read EMC 743

I Know My Colors

Red

3

Blue

4

Yellow

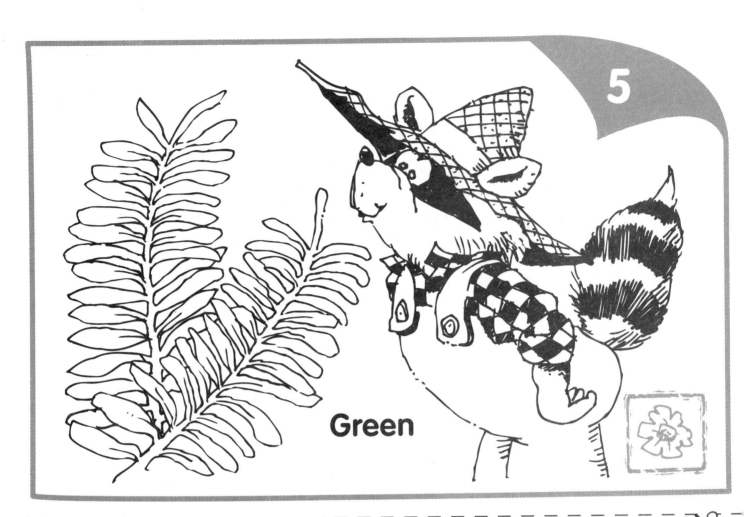

Green

Orange

Fifty Little Stories to Read EMC 743

7

Purple

8

Colors all around.

Fifty Little Stories to Read EMC 743

Boots

**Red boots, yellow boots,
blue boots, too.**

Which new boots belong to you?

Tall boots, short boots, narrow and wide.

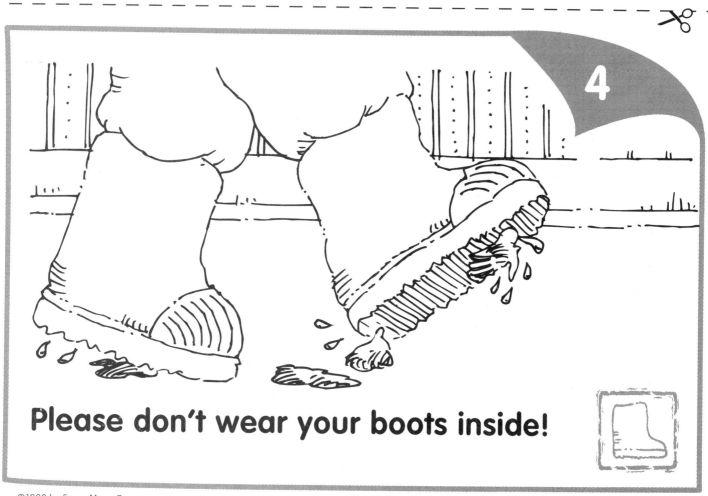

Please don't wear your boots inside!

A Celebration

**Sticks and mud and grass.
A robin's nest—first class.**

**Three tiny sky blue eggs
Tucked underneath her legs.**

**Mother Robin sits and waits.
Then, of course, she celebrates.**

Shoes

Sister wears dancing shoes.

Grandpa wears running shoes.

3

Mama wears dress-up shoes

4

and so do I!

 Fifty Little Stories to Read EMC 743

Camping

In a sleeping bag

In a tent

3

At the campground

4

In the forest

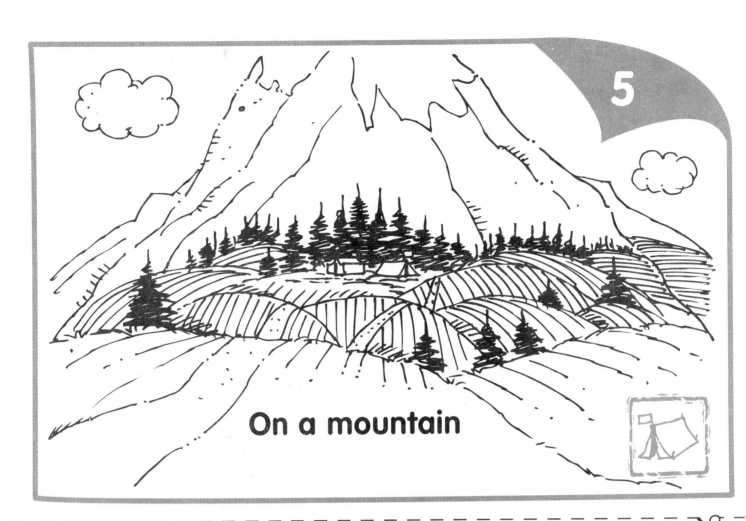

On a mountain

I'm camping.

Fifty Little Stories to Read EMC 743

The Walk

Along the sidewalk

There's a lot to see.

Won't you please come and

Take a walk with me.

Along the sidewalk

There's a lot to see.

I'm so glad that you

Took a walk with me.

My Frisbee

Throw it high.
Throw it low.
Watch it spin.
See it go.

Catch it high.
Catch it low.
Watch it spin.
See it go.

Playing frisbee with my friends—
Summer fun that never ends.

My Baby Brother

**Kicking feet
Tiny toes**

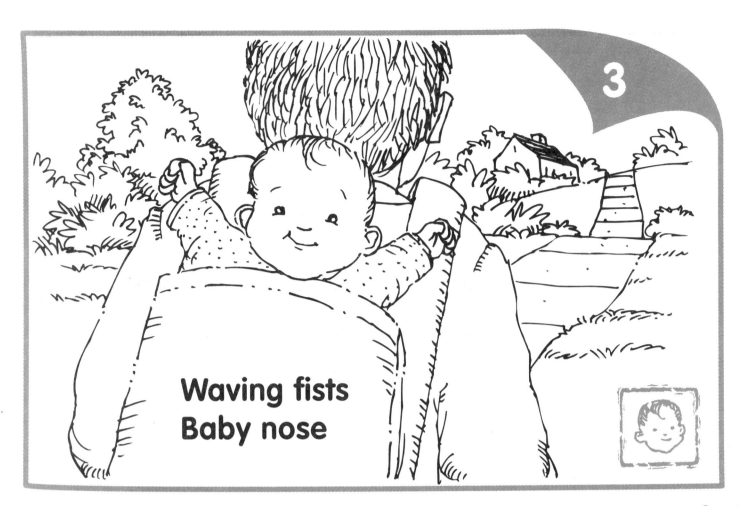

Waving fists
Baby nose

Soft pink cheeks
Round black eyes

 Fifty Little Stories to Read EMC 743

First he coos.
Then he cries.

Meet my baby brother.

The Builders

The builders dug a giant hole.

They made a wall of boards around the hole.

Fifty Little Stories to Read EMC 743

They filled the wall with cement.

They hammered new boards into the shape.

They put in windows and added a roof.

They built a new house for me.

Hiding

Mommy's looking for me.
Where am I hiding?

Brother's looking for me.
Where am I hiding?

Snickers is looking for me.
Where am I hiding?

Worms

In the garden
You disappear
Sliding away from me

Fifty Little Stories to Read EMC 743

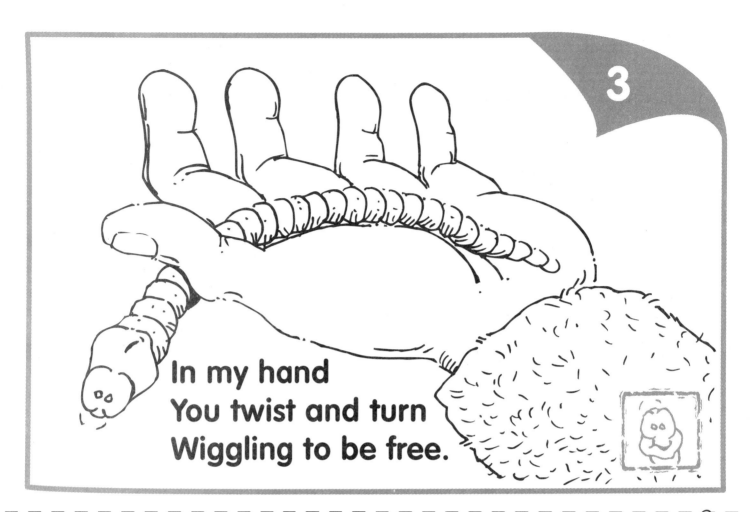

In my hand
You twist and turn
Wiggling to be free.

Squirm, Little Worm, squirm.

80 Fifty Little Stories to Read EMC 743

The Photographer

Stand up straight.

Look this way.

Move to the left.
Now to the right.

I like that great big smile.

My Treasure

I found it by the lake.
My treasure smooth and round.

I have it in my pocket.
That treasure that I found.

3

Would you like to see it?
I can show you if you like.

4

My treasure—it's a rock.
Isn't it a pretty sight?

Fifty Little Stories to Read EMC 743

Riding My Bike

Just start me off with a little push.
You needn't have any fear.

I learned to make the pedals work.
I turn the handlebars to steer.

How do I STOP?

I can ride all by myself!

When Auntie Comes

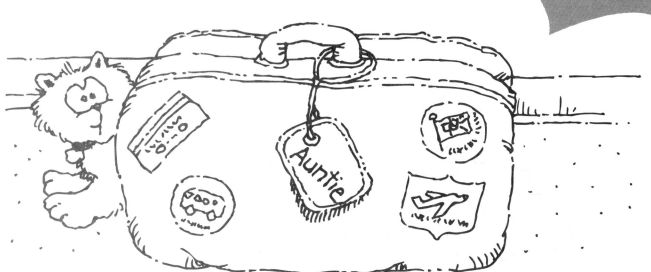

I'll sleep with Sis when Auntie comes.
I'll have to put away my shoes.

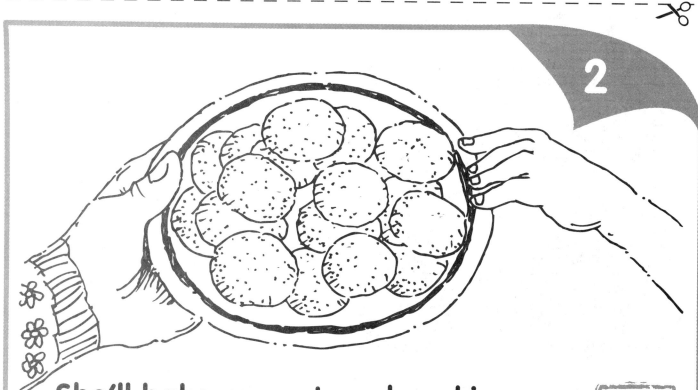

She'll bake me oatmeal cookies
To eat as we watch the news.

She'll nod and say
"My, how you've grown."
And then she'll pat my head and smile.

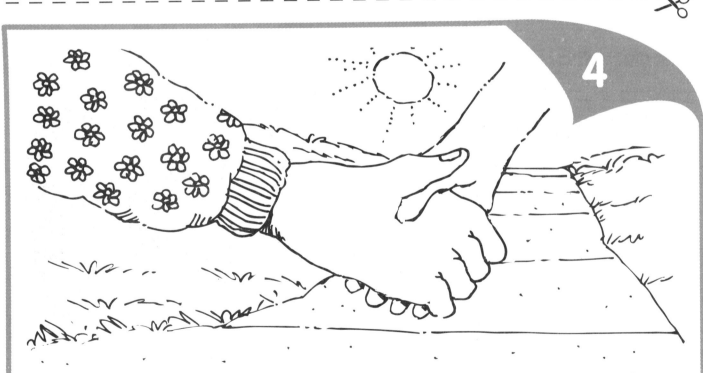

We'll take a walk. We'll smell a rose.
I hope that Auntie stays awhile.

1

2

The sky is black like Daddy's shiny shoes.

Fifty Little Stories to Read EMC 743

The stars shine bright like Nanna's ring.

My blanket's soft like Mother's hands.

Fifty Little Stories to Read EMC 743

5

I'll sip my cocoa. I'll read my book.
I'll snuggle down in bed.

6

The sky is black.
The stars shine bright.
My blanket's soft.
I'll say "Good night."

Fifty Little Stories to Read EMC 743

The Lost Tooth

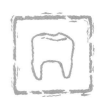

You won't believe what happened.
It was really a surprise.

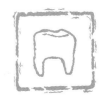

I opened up my mouth.
I couldn't believe my eyes.

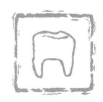

**My tooth was hanging loose,
Just holding at one side.**

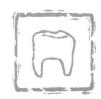

**I could push it back and forth.
I was really terrified.**

**It wiggled and it wiggled
There right next to my tongue.**

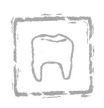

**I couldn't bear to pull it.
It sagged. It tipped. It hung.**

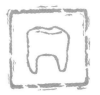

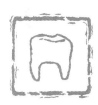

**Then when I ate a carrot
It popped out into my hand.**

**I lost a tooth! I lost a tooth!
And I am feeling grand.**

Put It All Together

one pumpkin

two eyes

Fifty Little Stories to Read EMC 743

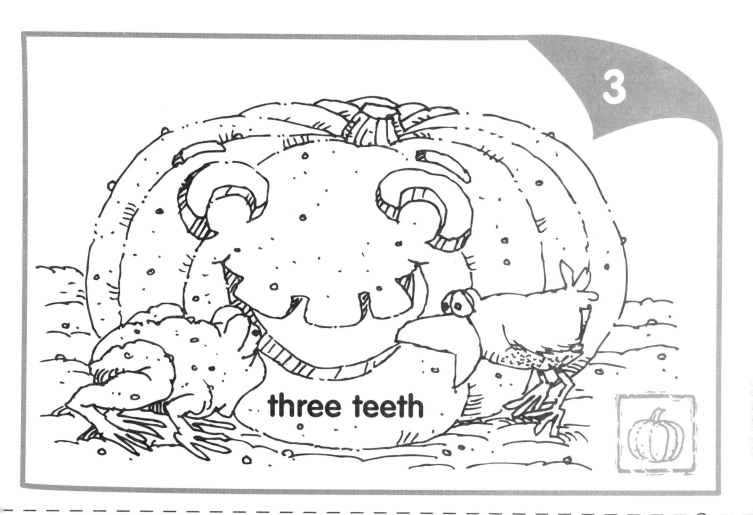

three teeth

Funny Jack-o-lantern!

Fifty Little Stories to Read EMC 743

What Are You Thankful For?

For sunshine and shade.
For games I have played.

Fifty Little Stories to Read EMC 743

For blankets at night.
And bear hugs tight.

What are you thankful for?

December Candles

Light the candles.

Light the candles.

Light the candles.

Candles light December nights.

Martin Luther King, Jr.

He had a special dream.

3

He worked to make it true.

4

He did it for all people,
including me and you.

Fifty Little Stories to Read EMC 743

George Washington and Abraham Lincoln—
Presidents from long ago,

2

They helped to make our country
The place that we all know.

3

We celebrate their birthdays
And remember them today.

4

Do you think that they would recognize
The good old U.S.A.?

Fifty Little Stories to Read EMC 743

Happy Spring

Birds are peeping.
Chicks are cheeping.

Gardens sprouting.
Children shouting.

It's spring!

 Fifty Little Stories to Read EMC 743

May Baskets

**Choose some flowers and a treat.
Put them down inside.**

**Set the basket near the door.
Ring the bell and hide.**

Happy May Day!

Summer Haircuts

Getting ready for summer.

Getting ready for summer.

Fifty Little Stories to Read EMC 743

Getting ready for summer.

Let's go!

Dear Mom and Dad,

I have this little story
About the things I do.
Please sit down and listen
I will read it now to you.

_____

_ _

_____
name